WELCOME—TO THE REST

You have just made the most imp[ortant decision of] your life. Now that you have don[e that, I want to] guide you as you think about what it means to become a Christian.

I once heard of a man who bought a ticket on a ship to cross the ocean. He had little money left, and so he stocked up on cheese and crackers to eat on the voyage. He dreamed of the good things that were waiting for him on the other side, and just endured the trip.

As the ship was docking, he told one of the ship's stewards that he had been eating cheese and crackers for two weeks. You can imagine his frustration when the steward said, "Didn't anyone tell you that all the buffets and huge meals were included in the price of your ticket?"

Like you, I'm looking forward to eternity with Christ. But, our Lord has an important feast for you to enjoy NOW. Don't miss out!

LET'S BEGIN WITH A REVIEW OF WHAT HAS HAPPENED TO YOU . . .

First of all, we want to talk about the word . . . GOD.

The Bible tells us He is POWERFUL. We usually don't have much problem believing that, do we? But, you should remember that His POWER is available for you! Scripture says He can heal our diseases, control circumstances, and release us from problems that have controlled us for years. Isn't that good news?

But we are also told God is PERSONAL. That's often a fact that we overlook. He loves you, and He wants you to think of Him as your Heavenly Father. If you have never been too close to your earthly father, this is good news for you. God loves you, and you don't have to do ONE SINGLE THING to make Him love you more. You are now His child, and He is going to care for you. He even knows the exact number of the hairs on your head!

Do you know how to talk to God? It's easy. People call it "prayer." Talk to God in the same way you share with someone you trust. Don't worry about whether He likes your choice of words or not—just talk to Him! He loves to hear you say that you love Him. He is pleased when you take time to just chat with Him about your life. In fact, if you learn to be silent some of the time as you talk to Him, you will quickly discover that He talks to you, too! You will hear His voice with your spiritual ears. (Please read John 3:1-16 in the New Testament.)

Next, we want to think about the word . . . MAN.

The Bible tells us that every one of us, without exception, has broken the tie God made to us when He created Adam and Eve. The results of that are really awful! In Romans 3:23 we are told that we have ALL sinned, and have ALL come short of God's glory.

It would be nice if we could convince ourselves that Man had a little "spark of goodness" in him that could be fanned into a flame. Unfortunately, that's not true.

Perhaps you have heard people say, "I keep the Ten Commandments as well as the next person." They think that impresses God. It doesn't! In fact, Isaiah wrote in chapter 64, verse 6, "All of us have become like one who is unclean, and all our RIGHTEOUS ACTS are like filthy rags; we all shrivel up like a leaf, and like the wind our sins sweep us away."

Did you notice that God considers even our RIGHTEOUS ACTS as a filthy rag? Whew! That's powerful. Even if we kept every single one of the Ten Commandments, He wouldn't be impressed. Lots of folks think they can DO something to make God love them. They have never learned that He already loves them. In fact, Romans 5:8 tells us that He demonstrates His love for us "While we were still sinners." Jesus Christ is God, and He died for us. That's how we know!

To understand man's problem, we must consider the word . . . SIN.

Here are a couple of men walking along. In the background is a tree. Let's imagine this tree is an APPLE tree (notice the round apples all over it).

QUESTION:
Do we call the tree "APPLE" because it has fruit on it called "APPLES?"

Or, do we say it bears "APPLES" because it's an "APPLE" tree?

Obviously, if it's not fruit-bearing time, the tree is not a PEACH tree, is it? The right answer to the question is . . . it bears "APPLES" because it's an APPLE tree!

That brings us to the word SIN.

It doesn't have the same meaning as the word SINS.

4

SIN *is a root word, and* SINS *is a "fruit" word.*

Man's problem isn't primarily related to the FRUIT of his life; his problem is at the ROOT of his life! He has a SIN problem.

SIN

Let's look at the root of a Man's life. The Bible refers to it as our "HEART." To say it simply, man has a HEART PROBLEM.

In this diagram, we see a tree with ROOTS and FRUITS. Beside it is a HEART, the root of Man. Within that heart, there's a throne and a crown. Around the outside of the heart are the FRUITS that come from the ROOT.

Do you have a pen nearby? Draw an "X" over the "S" and "N" in the diagram. Then, draw an "I" on the throne, wearing the crown. That's the way the Bible defines "SIN." It's a condition in which you and I have declared ourselves to be the master—the king—the owner—the "boss"—of our own lives. You see, that's what makes us unacceptable to God. He never intended for us to own ourselves!

In fact this total rebellion against God's ownership of us brings WRATH.

Romans 2:5 says, "But because of your stubbornness and your unrepentant heart, you are storing up wrath against yourself for the day of God's wrath, when his righteous judgment will be revealed."

Some people want to avoid this point, saying that God's love cancels out "wrath." But, if we look at what this verse is saying, we realize that WE are the ones STORING UP WRATH FOR OURSELVES. God isn't doing it to US; we are doing it OURSELVES!

If a man commits murder, do we accuse the judge of being unreasonable when the sentence is declared and the man is condemned? Of course not! The murderer was personally responsible for his destiny.

Thus, we discover that Man has caused a terrible problem for himself. He tries to find a way to "patch things up" with God. Here is a check list for you to consider. How many of them have you, yourself, tried in the past?

☐ WENT TO CHURCH
☐ DID GOOD WORKS
☐ TRIED OTHER RELIGIONS

HERE'S A LITTLE PICTURE THAT DESCRIBES THE PROBLEM OF MAN . . .

This poor fellow began to swim across a lake. Of course, he was confident when he started that he could accomplish his goal. He needed no help. But now, something terrible has happened—a cramp in his side has made it impossible for him to swim. He's in trouble!

Let's imagine for a moment that he makes a decision to "keep his problem to himself" and "find his own solution." How long is he going to last before he drowns? He realizes he has no choice, and cries out, "HELP!" Unless someone comes to save him, he's doomed. Fortunately, he is willing to admit he has a problem. Because of this, there is a possibility that someone who is nearby will rescue him.

WHAT KIND OF A PERSON WILL BE REQUIRED TO SAVE HIM?

First of all, it will have to be someone who is able to share his environment—in this case, water.

Second, this person will have to be strong enough to care for his own needs, PLUS meeting the needs of the drowning man. Such a savior may not be easy to find!

A SAVIOR COMES TO RESCUE HIM . . .

and, safe on the bank, he now shares his thanks with the one who rescued him.

QUESTION: IN THE CASE OF THIS MAN, WHAT "ELEMENT" WAS GOING TO CAUSE HIS DEATH?

Obviously, it was the WATER that was going to destroy him. He was not created with lungs to breathe underwater like a fish. He was out of his "element," and thus faced sudden destruction.

In the illustration on this page, the "element" that is about to destroy Man is "SIN." Note the "I" is made larger than the "S" and "N" to remind us that it is the source of our problem.

Did you understand all this when you made your decision to accept Jesus Christ a little while ago? Did you understand that Jesus is the ONLY SAVIOR who has the ability to rescue us? Acts 4:12 says, "Salvation is found in NO ONE ELSE, for there is no other name under heaven given to men by which we must be saved."

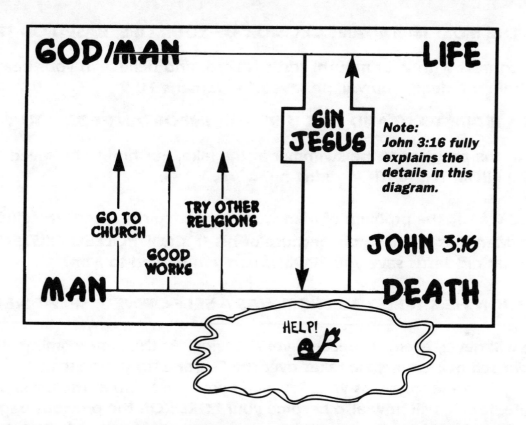

Luke 19:10 tells us, "For the Son of Man (Jesus) came to seek and to save what was lost." In this illustration, YOU are the one He sought and saved! Thank Him for doing so right now. Tell Him of your love for Him!

YOU MADE THE MOST IMPORTANT DECISION OF YOUR LIFE, BASED ON THIS TRUTH:

"That if you confess with your mouth, Jesus is Lord, and believe in your heart that God raised Him from the dead, you will be saved."— Romans 10:9.

BUT THERE'S MORE TO IT, AND THIS IS REALLY IMPORTANT FOR YOU TO KNOW!

Let's return to the problem of the swimmer in the lake. For him to be saved, he had to be REMOVED FROM THE WATER, didn't he?

. . . What did we say the problem of Man was? As we "spiritualized" the illustration, we realized that Man was going to die because of his "I" CONTROLLED EXISTENCE. Therefore: what did Jesus save you FROM when you prayed to Him?

THE CONDITION HE SAVED YOU FROM WAS A SELF-OWNED, SELF-DIRECTED LIFE.

You see, He will never, ever just become your "Savior." At the very moment He saves you from your self-owned life, He takes over the "Throne" in your "Heart." It cost Him his life on Calvary to come to you as your Savior. As you meet Him at the Cross, it will cost you YOUR life, for He will now also become your LORD! On the previous page, you noticed that one side of the Cross had an arrow pointing downward. That described His journey to earth to save you. It was a costly journey, for He took all your sin upon Himself. 1 Peter 2:24 says, "He Himself bore our sins in His body on the tree, so that we might die to sins and live for righteousness; by His wounds you have been healed."

10

WHY NOT TAKE A MOMENT RIGHT NOW TO GIVE JESUS THE COMPLETE RIGHT TO BE NOT ONLY SAVIOR, BUT ALSO THE LORD AND MASTER OF YOUR LIFE?

Pray, "Jesus, all I know about myself I give to all I know about You!"

Those who become Christians without this total surrender of their life to His Lordship don't do well. In fact, the writer of Hebrews in the New Testament describes them as "freaks" who act like babies when they should be mature and strong in their faith-walk (Hebrews 5:12-14). It's important that you settle this matter right now.

YOU WILL NOW BEGIN THE MOST EXCITING PART OF YOUR ENTIRE LIFE!

As you presented your life to Jesus Christ, He immediately placed His presence within you! You will never be alone again. But there is another truth you must know: Jesus has also entered other persons around you and has joined you to them. Together with them, you now become the body of Christ, "called-out ones." You will gather with them in home groups, building up one another and also revealing His presence with those who do not know about Him.

Those who have given you this little booklet are members of a "Cell Group." By joining their group, your life will be strengthened by believers who will seek to guide you through the stages of spiritual growth that follow your decision. Apart from this relationship, you will never discover the freedom from the power of sin that Christ desires for you to experience.

The Bible describes your present need: ". . . like newborn babies, crave pure spiritual milk, so that by it you may grow up in your salvation." (1 Peter 2:2). Involve yourself immediately in a Cell Group. Consider it your spiritual family. You will find more mature believers in it, who will minister to you. More important, as you attend the weekly Cell meetings, you'll observe the way more mature Christians live and serve. They will be good "models" for you to observe.

CELL GROUPS: THE "HAPPY HOUR" IN THE CHRISTIAN LIFE

There's an event unbelievers look forward to, often called the "Happy Hour." It's a time when friends get together for an hour or so and drink alcoholic spirits to "get happy." Perhaps you have shared in such events? Christians have the only TRUE "Happy Hour!" It's a special time, called a "Cell Group," when they get together to be with their Lord.

In Ephesians 5:18 Paul writes, "Do not get drunk on wine, which leads to debauchery. Instead, be filled with the Spirit. Speak to one another with psalms, hymns and spiritual songs. Sing and make music in your heart to the Lord, always giving thanks to God the Father for everything, in the name of our Lord Jesus Christ."

As you grow in your new life, your Cell Group will be a weekly "Happy Hour" when you relax with fellow believers. It's a time for sharing joys and problems. In your midst is the Christ Who dwells IN you. He's the One who fills the time with His presence and His power. It is in these gatherings that you will be ministered to by others. You see, He will usually come through a fellow Christian to meet your need— and He will flow through YOU to meet another person's need!

Your Cell Leader will visit you very soon after you attend the first Cell Group. In preparation for this, he or she will give you a JOURNEY GUIDE to thoughtfully read through before the visit. Together, you will then chart a "Spiritual Journey" to help you grow into the completeness of your Christian life. Another Cell member will become your "Sponsor" as you get acquainted with your Bible and discover the spiritual gifts which now reside within you.

As your prayer life deepens and you share in the Cell Group times, you will discover how to use the gifts of the Spirit to build up others and to share your faith with your friends who are not Christians. Spiritual "gifts" are not the same thing as your "talents." The gifts of the Spirit are provided to you by the Christ who lives within you. He will use you to perform His work as you open yourself to serve Him.

You will truly cherish the times you attend a "Celebration Service," where the combined Cells meet together to worship their Lord. Your Cell Group Church will also have some special "Weekends" for you to attend to help you grow spiritually. Also, there are self-study materials which will be used by you daily and then reviewed during the Cell

Group Equipping Times. Your growth in Christ should be constant: active participation in the Cell Group meetings and the equipping guides will insure it!

WHY THE CELL GROUP IS CRUCIAL TO YOUR NEW LIFE IN CHRIST

James 5:16 tells us to confess our sins to each other and pray for each other so that we may be healed. The secret to breaking the power of sin in our lives is becoming responsible and accountable to others in the body of Christ. Confessing our sins unlocks the deep issues of our heart, and humility holds the door open so heart change can occur.

In the Cell Group, pride and sin are stripped of their power, no longer able to control our lives. You will quickly discover that not only are you strengthened by the encouragement of the group, but that you also will be given God's strengthening words for others. Thus, you will grow both by being helped and by helping others. It is only when we are sharing with other Christians we know well that we discover how to overcome the power of sin in our lives. It cannot be done in isolation from the body of Christ!

On the next page, there's a Covenant for you to sign. May God guide your every step!

My Personal Covenant

Knowing that Christ has brought me
His peace, I will declare Him to be
Lord over all my life.
My body, my possessions, and my future
are His to command.
I will join my life to a Cell Group and
consider it my Basic Christian Community.
I will respond to all with God's acceptance.
I will not be judgmental.
I will always remember that God allows all
things for His eternal purposes.
I will learn to pray and seek to know how
to hear His voice speaking to me.
I will prayerfully seek to know what,
in each situation, God wants to address,
And be His instrument of healing.

Knowing that my Cell Group may be a
turning point for my life or that of another
person, I covenant to place my commitment
to its ministry at the very top
of my priority list.
As God anoints me, I shall be His
instrument to save, to heal, to deliver, and
to restore others.
In this spirit, I invite His Spirit to take my
life and use it for His glory.

_____

Name

_____

Date

HOW TO MAKE TIME TO BE WITH YOUR BEST FRIEND . . .

Perhaps you have never thought about Jesus, the Son of God, becoming your "best friend," but that's exactly what He wants to be to you. In John 15:15 He said, ". . . I have called you friends, for everything that I learned from my Father I have made known to you."

Proverbs 18:24 tells us "there is a friend who sticks closer than a brother." That's Jesus! Don't think of Him as a God who is "up there." Paul said in Galatians 2:20, "I have been crucified with Christ and I no longer live, but CHRIST LIVES IN ME. The life I live in the body, I live by faith in the Son of God, who loved me and gave himself for me."

Isn't that tremendous? When you realize that CHRIST IS IN YOU, you never have to "get together" with Him. You ARE together! Discover the wonderful experience of sharing your thoughts, your working hours, your problems, your joys, with Him. He is never distant from you. HE IS WITHIN YOU.

In the same way that "best friends" often take a break to share a cup of coffee or tea and just talk, you will want to take time to be with Him during a special time each day.

He will share many new thoughts with you as you read your Bible during these moments. His Spirit will make scripture truths very, very personal to you. It's not disrespectful to think of Him as though He were sitting across the table from you!

We recommend you take some time during each day to spend time with Him. Mornings are great for some people, evenings are better for others. Set your own schedule, but then seek to be with Him EACH DAY. Talk to Him, and listen as He talks to you. Above all, LEARN TO ENJOY BEING WITH HIM!

Your Bible can be very useful during these times, but don't turn your time with Him into a Bible study time. He wants you to enjoy HIS presence. You will be helped to learn all about your Bible as you enter Cell Group life. In fact, you will be helped to spend a whole year surveying it. But, your Friend wants you to be with HIM.

The words "listening room" are used to describe your fellowship with Him. Some of the things you may want to include are: worshipping Him; praying about situations in the lives of your Cell Group members; praying for your national leadership; praying for friends who are not believers; praying for your family members; and, finally, praying for your own needs. As you talk to Him, be certain He will also give His words to you.

HIDING GOD'S WRITTEN WORD IN YOUR HEART

There are times when a scripture verse is very important to meet a need in your life. Unfortunately, we can't walk around with a Bible open all day long! That's why, for many centuries, believers have memorized special scripture portions. You have such passages available at all times, in all situations.

Psalm 119:11 says, "I have hidden your word in my heart that I might not sin against you." You have an enemy who is going to attack you in the days ahead. Satan isn't happy about losing you! He enjoyed guiding your journey to eternal destruction, and strongly dislikes the fact that you will now enjoy eternity with Christ. His greatest attacks are going to come to you now. Your best defense against him is God's written word, hidden in your heart.

On the next page is a special set of verses for you to memorize. On one side of the page is the verse; on the other side is the reference. Learn to remember where the verse is found in your Bible by letting the reference prompt your recall of the text. You will find that these verses are easy to memorize if you read them aloud several times before you go to bed each night and then again first thing in the morning.

As you enter your "Year of Equipping" in the Cell Group, additional scripture verses will be included in each portion of your study. Keep increasing your memorized scriptures—and remember to review them constantly!

And this is the testimony: God has given us eternal life, and this life is in his Son. He who has the Son has life; he who does not have the Son of God does not have life.

1 JOHN 5:11-12

If we confess our sins, he is faithful and just and will forgive us our sins and purify us from all unrighteousness.

1 JOHN 1:9

Until now you have not asked for anything in my name. Ask and you will receive, and your joy will be complete.

JOHN 16:24

For though we live in the world, we do not wage war as the world does. The weapons we fight with are not the weapons of the world. On the contrary, they have divine power to demolish strongholds.

2 CORINTHIANS 10:3-4

No temptation has seized you except what is common to man. And God is faithful: He will not let you be tempted beyond what you can bear. But when you are tempted, He will also provide a way out so that you can stand up under it.

1 CORINTHIANS 10:13

Trust in the LORD with all your heart and lean not on your own understanding; in all your ways acknowledge him, and he will make your paths straight.

PROVERBS 3:5-6

1 JOHN 5:11-12

1 JOHN 1:9

JOHN 16:24

2 CORINTHIANS 10:3-4

1 CORINTHIANS 10:13

PROVERBS 3:5-6